THE BEST
BAPTISM EVER

THE BEST BAPTISM EVER

Jake's Story

by Bette Molgard

Bookcraft
Salt Lake City, Utah

To my second-grade students at
East Elementary
Tooele, Utah

Library of Congress Catalog Card Number: 93-71290
ISBN 0-88494-880-3

Second Printing, 1995

Printed in the United States of America

CHAPTER

THE GREAT
KAHUNA

I was just dozing off. Dad and I were fishing on the Snake River below Jackson Hole, Wyoming—our favorite fishing spot. We have a silver rubber raft. It isn't very big, but it's just right for Dad and me.

Early that morning we'd floated over to the side of the river across from the road. We'd fished for a few hours partway down the river until we had hit our favorite fishing hole. Dad had caught two nice ones, but I had only had a few nibbles all day. Now I was sitting on the damp, sandy shore. My fishing hat shaded my face from the bright sun, but the rest of my body could feel its warm rays. I leaned back, closed my eyes, and listened to the quiet roar of the river.

The jerky nibbles as the fish sampled my worm brought me back. My eyes popped open and my mind was immediately wide awake. I waited until the fish had really taken the bait before I jerked the pole, cinching the hook. The whir of the reel sent excitement through my body, and I stood up to reel in my fish.

It was a big fish, I could tell, and I didn't want to lose him in the battle to get him to shore. I used all the tips Dad had taught me and all my fishing experience. I could hear Dad's words in my mind just as if he were standing beside me. "Don't let it come out of the water, or you'll lose it. Don't reel too fast, or the hook will come out of its mouth; but reel fast enough that the line doesn't slacken." I'd heard them often enough. We had been fishing partners since I was two.

There's nothing in the world more exciting than catching a fish, and by the time I got my fish to the shore my heart was pounding with excitement. It was a big fish, just as I had thought, and as I took out the hook I glanced up the river through the trees to see if Dad had watched the show. Sure enough, he gave me the thumbs-up sign. I held the fish up with a grin. The river was noisy, but words didn't have to be exchanged. We had both had a great day of fishing, and, as Grandma Tolson always says, that's "pure living."

I put the fish in my green creel, put another worm on my hook, and was then ready for another fish to make my afternoon exciting. Dad hiked over the rock ledge that separated us, took a small cooler out of the raft, and sat down to share a shore lunch. I could tell it was a shore lunch. Dad always makes lunch on our fishing days, and those lunches aren't anything like Mom's, that I take to school. This lunch had pop, candy, crackers, cheese, chips, and an orange. There were sandwiches, and more candy to put in my fanny pack to nibble on all afternoon. Dads really know how to pack a lunch!

We nibbled and sipped and fished until the cool breeze and long shadows said our fishing day was over. Dad said we had just enough time to float down the rapids before dark, so we got in the raft and drifted toward the first set of rapids. Our raft has metal bars across the middle, wooden seats, and a metal part on each side that holds the oars. With this setup Dad can row all by himself, and I just have to sit back and enjoy the ride.

We'd been down this river lots of times. There was only one part that made me nervous, and that's the Great Kahuna. It's the biggest rapid and is almost like falling over a waterfall. Right after the Great Kahuna is Lunch Counter, another big one, and then the rest of the river trip is full of smaller rapids. The Kahuna and Lunch Counter are usually fun, and I had never told Dad that they scared me, but I was always glad when we were past those two rapids.

I could hear\the Kahuna roar before we rounded the last curve of the river. There were a lot of other rafts ahead of us on the river, and one by one they disappeared in front of us as the Kahuna swallowed them and then waited for its next victim. I could hear the people screaming, but as we got closer we could see over the edge that all the other rafts really had made it past Kahuna. Dad told me to get down low in the boat and hang on to the metal bars. He lined the boat up straight, and soon we were over the edge of Kahuna.

I screamed. I couldn't help it—it's something that my body does automatically when I'm scared to death. We made it over the edge, down the waterfall, but as we got to the bottom of Kahuna the top of the raft straightened out and then kept going. The whole raft came over the top of us, and Dad and I were both swallowed by the churning water.

I looked around in a panic. I couldn't see anything, and couldn't tell which way was up and which way was down. I couldn't see Dad or the boat. I was all alone under the water.

The second I thought I was all alone, I heard Mom's voice in my mind saying, "No matter where you are, no matter what you're doing, Heavenly Father is with you, and will answer your prayers." This would be the true test. If He could hear me when I was under water in the middle of the Kahuna, He could hear anyone, anytime. I quickly said in my mind, "Heavenly Father, help me!"

It was just as if a hand was pulling me. My life-jacket popped me up on the other side of the churning, and a man in another raft told me to grab onto his oar. In no time at all I was in his raft.

"Jake! Jake! Over here!" I looked around to see Dad over on the shore. I found out later that he had come up faster than I had and was right beside the boat. He hung on to the boat and kicked until he was by the shore. The group of people that stand on the rocks and watch people go through Kahuna had helped him get the raft out of the water while he watched for me to come up. It had all taken just a few seconds, but it had seemed like one of those funny slow-motion pictures. We were glad when we got together again, and were extra glad that we had tied the oars to the boat so that they hadn't floated on down the river. We got back into the boat, pushed off, and went down the rest of the river with no problem.

Bouncing along in the old green truck that evening, wrapped in the green army blanket, I thought about how fast Heavenly Father had heard me. I told Dad about my prayer, and he said that he had prayed too. He put his arm around me and gave me a squeeze. I felt warm all over and was extra happy that night that I had two fathers, my Heavenly Father and my earthly father, who loved me.

A NEW FRIEND

When the weekend was over I was back in school. I'm in the second grade at East Elementary, in Mrs. Barker's class. I think there are only two good things about school. I like lunch and I like recess. It's not that I have trouble doing the regular school things—I can read, and I'm really good at math. But to have to try to sit still that long makes me crazy.

I know some people don't have that problem. My twin sister, Jenny, likes every part of school. She never gets in trouble, and she sits still and doesn't talk.

Talking to Danny was the only thing that made going to school the rest of the day fun. But our second grade teacher doesn't understand. Mrs. Barker thinks we should go the whole day without talking to anyone except during lunch and during recess.

I don't think I've ever made it. I've been moved lots of times while Mrs. Barker tried to decide where I could sit and be quiet.

That Monday I was sitting by Danny, and we were talking while Mrs. Barker wrote our spelling words on the board. We'd already had our warning, but we both thought it wouldn't hurt to talk when we weren't expected to be doing anything else. I thought I would just be sent to the trouble desk, but Mrs. Barker really lost her temper. She yelled at us and then told me to move all my things back into the empty desk next to Elwood Blackendorf.

Elwood was a new kid in school. As soon as he came to our school kids started making fun of him. His ears are huge. I'd never seen any ears quite like them. Neither had anyone else, so from the first day everyone started to call him Dumbo. They never did it in front of Mrs. Barker, of course, but when an adult wasn't listening, Elwood was called Dumbo.

I had never called him Dumbo. I had never really called him anything; he was just an extra person that sat at the back of my class. But the day Mrs. Barker sat me beside him I had to get to know him. I couldn't just sit and be quiet, and he was the only person I could talk to.

By lunchtime I knew that I had made a new friend. Elwood, my old desk partner, Danny, and I went outside to play after lunch. Danny asked us if we wanted to see something that he had taken from his Dad's dresser before he had left for school. We went over by the fence where no one could see us, and there he showed us some matches. We knew we weren't supposed to play with matches, but we wanted to see if we could just catch something on fire. It was stupid, but it wasn't the first stupid thing

I'd done. We looked around to see what we could burn, but everything was kind of wet. The grass had just been watered by the sprinkling system, but there were some leaves that looked dry that had been caught in the fence.

Elwood, Danny, and I sat kind of in a circle and piled the leaves in the middle. There was a little breeze blowing, so we cupped our hands around the little flame the match made. I'd seen Dad do that on our camping trips. We had just gotten a little fire going when Elwood saw a third-grade kid walking toward us. That's when we realized that we were doing a stupid thing. We all knew that if the kid saw what we were doing and told the teacher on recess duty, we would be in real trouble. We'd all three end up going to the principal's office. My mind couldn't think of anything to do that would solve our problem, and the fire was getting bigger. Danny didn't think of anything, either. We just sat there trying to hide the fire behind us as the kid came closer and closer.

But Elwood saved the day. He stood up behind us just before the kid got to us, then quickly sat down on the fire. His pants were wet from the wet lawn, and we heard a little sizzling sound as he sat. The fire was now out, and we looked at the third-grade kid as if nothing had happened. He asked us if we had seen his ball. When we told him no, he turned around and went back to where he had come from.

We all three let out a big sigh. It had been a close call! Elwood stood up to check whether he had burned his pants—that could have been embarrassing. But his pants were just a little black and there weren't any burn holes. He sat down and tried to rub the black into the wet grass. When he stood up again, his pants were a little less black, but we couldn't tell whether that was because he had rubbed some off or whether the grass stains covered up the black. Either way, his mom wasn't going to be happy.

The bell rang, and Danny and I gave Elwood a high five and ran to line up at the door. The three of us stood in the back of the line. Elwood didn't want anyone making fun of the back of his pants. We kind of sneaked into our seats at the back of the class and quietly waited for Mrs. Barker to start handing out the timed tests for math.

Jenny sat at the front of the class. She doesn't like timed tests but I do. When the timed tests were over, Jenny started to cry. I hate it when she cries. She worries about everything. Mom says she needs to put the two of us together, shake us up, and then maybe we'd worry just right. I never worry about anything.

But this time Jenny really did have something to worry about. I think even I would have been worried. She had borrowed our older sister Monica's necklace that morning for good luck on the timed test. Jenny had been stuck on +4's forever and so badly wanted to pass them that she knew she needed extra luck. Monica hadn't wanted her to wear the necklace, but when Jenny begged her Monica said she could wear it for one day. And she'd better not lose it.

Monica is fourteen and kind of scary. We like her, but she gets mad really easy, and she was mad that morning just thinking about what she'd do to Jenny if she didn't bring her necklace back after school. Jenny had promised she'd take good care of it, and when Jenny promises, you know she's going to keep her promise. That's just how Jenny is.

But Monica's necklace was gone. Jenny didn't know where she had lost it, but she knew that if she didn't find it she'd have to face Monica. Mrs. Barker told her to go outside and look for it, and she let Jenny's friend Jamie go along to help. But when they came in they hadn't found it on the playground or in the lost and found.

Later, during art, Jenny came back to my desk to borrow her red crayon. I always lose my crayons, and Jenny always has all the colors, so I had borrowed hers the last time we'd had art. While she was getting her crayon she saw Monica's necklace in the tray of Elwood's desk.

Jenny didn't know that Elwood was my friend and that we had spent all recess together. She just knew that she wanted Monica's necklace back. She said, "Elwood! You have my necklace in your desk!"

Mrs. Barker stood right up and walked fast back to Elwood. "Elwood, do you have Jenny's necklace?" she asked.

"No. . . . I mean—it was in my desk, but I didn't take it." I could tell that Elwood was scared. Everyone is scared when Mrs. Barker gets mad.

"Then how did it get into your desk? Did it walk there from outside? You are really in the hot seat now, young man!"

Mrs. Barker was mad. But when she said "hot seat," all I could think about was Elwood sitting on the fire and sizzling. I about exploded in trying to keep from laughing.

When she told him that he had to stay in from recess for a week and write sentences, it dawned on me that Elwood couldn't have put Monica's necklace in his desk. I had been with him all recess. I was afraid to say anything—Mrs. Barker mustn't know about what we had done at recess. But someone was trying to get Elwood in trouble. Nobody really liked him, but nobody really knew him. I wasn't sure what to do. All I knew was that we'd had too much fun at recess to miss a whole week while Elwood wrote sentences.

TWIN TALK

That evening I went into Jenny's bedroom just before dark. She was reading on her bed but scooted over so I could sit down.

I knew I could trust Jenny not to tell anyone what I was going to tell her. We'd had twin secrets before and no one ever found out.

I got up and looked down the hall to make sure no one could hear, then I started to talk very quietly.

"Jenny," I said, "Elwood didn't take your necklace. I don't know who did, but it wasn't Elwood. I think someone put it in his desk just to get him into trouble."

"How do you know that?" she asked.

"Because I was with him all recess."

"Well, then, why didn't you tell Mrs. Barker that when she got mad at him?" she asked me, but I could tell that she already knew the answer. Anyone would be afraid to say anything to Mrs. Barker when she was mad like that. But I had a much better reason.

"Because I was afraid we were all going to be in trouble if I said anything."

"Why?"

"Because Danny brought some matches to school. His dad smokes, and he just took some of his dad's matches. Elwood was with us the whole recess. He's not so bad, Jenny."

I told her all about the fire and how Elwood had saved the day. Jenny's laugh always starts out with a snicker and gets bigger and bigger until she sounds kind of like a machine gun. That's exactly what happened this time. I guess the picture in her mind as she thought about Elwood sitting on the fire and sizzling was so funny she couldn't stop laughing. Her laugh is contagious, and pretty soon she got me laughing so hard that I thought both of us were going to fall off the bed.

We finally settled down, and Jenny asked, "But if Elwood was with you, how did Monica's necklace get in his desk?"

"I don't know. You know how everyone is mean to him. They never even look at anything but his ears. But I played with him today, Jenny, and I like him. I think someone was just trying to get him in trouble. If Elwood had wanted to keep it, it wouldn't have been right in the front of his desk. He would have hidden it."

"Well, I still don't like him. Nobody likes him, Jake. Everyone will think you're weird like he is if you're his friend. I wish you weren't his friend. It would be a whole lot easier. But you're right. Dumbo probably didn't take Monica's necklace."

Jenny used Elwood's nickname and I didn't like that. But I was glad that at least she knew he hadn't taken Monica's necklace.

We talked some more, and we decided that I should tell Mrs. Barker in the morning that Elwood had been with me all recess. She didn't need to know what we had been doing. We just didn't want Elwood in trouble for something he hadn't done.

I was glad I'd talked to Jenny. She's not very good at timed tests, but she is great at helping to figure out real life problems.

WHO'S GOING TO BAPTIZE US?

The next morning at breakfast Mom reminded us that we needed to choose who was to baptize us in a couple of weeks.

Mom is a Mormon, but Dad isn't. He's a great dad, but he couldn't baptize us. We needed to find someone who held the priesthood. My Primary teacher said that an angel had given the priesthood to John the Baptist, and Jesus gave it to Peter, James, and John. Then these men gave the priesthood to Joseph Smith. And Joseph Smith gave the priesthood to men in The Church of Jesus Christ of Latter-day Saints. Everyone in our church who holds the priesthood can tell how his priesthood goes back to Jesus. When I get to be twelve, I'll hold the priesthood.

But right then I was turning eight, and I needed to choose someone to baptize me. Jenny asked Monica who had baptized her. She said it was done by

Grandpa Tolson. She told us it was so neat. She even remembered how special she had felt as she came out of the water. Then the next day, Grandpa Tolson had confirmed her. But Grandpa Tolson had died last year. We asked Mom who else could baptize us.

Mom thought for a minute, then she said, "Well, there's Uncle John or Bishop Lee—or Brother Henderson."

That was a lot to think over. I knew I would never choose Brother Henderson. He's our home teacher. He comes to our home at the end of every month and shakes Mom's hand and says, "Good evening, Sister Jacobs," and then he shakes Dad's hand and says, "Good evening, Brother Jacobs." Dad hates to be called Brother Jacobs. He's even said that to Mom. But he's always nice to Brother Henderson.

After shaking hands, Brother Henderson sits down and asks us how we all are. Then he doesn't know what to say next, so there's always a big quiet time until Mom thinks of something. Then another long quiet time until Mom thinks of something else to say. His visits seem as long as first reading group, our class just before recess at school.

Bishop Lee is nice, but I didn't know him very well because he'd only been our bishop for three months. I would have my interview with him that evening.

Jenny decided to ask Uncle Jerry, Mom's brother. He just started going to church last year. Before that, Mom said, he wasn't living the way Heavenly Father wanted him to live. Then he was in a motorcycle accident. He's in a wheelchair now, but he's doing a lot of things right. I thought it would be great if he baptized Jenny. Uncle Jerry had never baptized anyone before.

But Uncle John had always been my favorite uncle. When I was born, Uncle John said I should have been his kid. We have the same bright red hair and the same freckles all over the place. When I was a little kid, Uncle John would come over and lift me up, hold my face next to his, and say, "Who can tell which one is Jake and which one is Uncle John?"

Everyone would act as if they couldn't tell which was which and Uncle John and I would laugh because we'd tricked them again.

A favorite uncle was just right. I decided to ask Uncle John to baptize me.

THE INTERVIEW

That evening we were to have the bishop's interview. He had to talk to us to make sure we knew everything we had to know to be baptized. Jenny was really worried (again!). She just knew that she was going to be the only person ever to get an F in the bishop's interview. I wasn't worried at all. I figured that if I didn't know something I needed to know, the bishop would tell me it.

When we first got to the church the bishop was talking to someone else in his office, so we sat down on the padded bench outside his office to wait. Jenny, Mom, my baby sister, Doodles, and I sat there for a few minutes, but Doodles couldn't handle sitting still for very long. In just a few minutes she jumped down and ran towards the front foyer beside the chapel.

Doodles is just one and a half years old. I think

her name is cool. It's not her real name. Her real name is Amy, but the first sound she made was "Dooo, dooo, dooo," so everyone calls her Doodles. We should have named her Trouble. She gets in trouble more than I do!

Mom knew I didn't like to sit still, so she sent me to find out what Doodles was up to. The minute I found her, I knew I was too late. She had climbed up on the back of one of the couches in the foyer and had been able to reach the little papers you fill out when you pay your tithing; and the envelopes too. There was a little mountain of envelopes on the couch and another little mountain on the floor, with pieces scattered here and there. "Doodles!" I said, and she jumped. Then she grabbed the last handful of envelopes and hung on as she turned away from me. She must have known she was in trouble.

Mom had heard me, and she came quickly to help clean up the mess. Jenny was right behind her. Doodles was not happy that we had stopped her fun, so all the noise let the bishop know where we were when he left his office and found the bench empty.

"Who wants to be first for their baptism interview?" he asked. "How about the oldest?"

I had been born two whole minutes before Jenny, so I jumped up from my clean-up duty and went with the bishop. Jenny was so scared, she didn't want to be first anyway, and I was glad to leave her and Mom to clean up the envelope mountain.

The bishop closed the door and asked me to sit down in the big wooden chair in front of his desk. After taking his seat, he said, "Jake, why do you want to be baptized?"

"Well," I replied, "I want to be a member of Jesus' true church."

"I'm sure you do. It's a very special church. It's the only church that has permission from Jesus to be His church. Do you know why you have to wait until you're eight to be baptized instead of getting baptized when you're a baby?"

I knew that answer. My Primary teacher had talked about baptism a lot during the year. "Eight is how old you are when Heavenly Father knows you can be counted on to know what is wrong and what is right."

"That's exactly right, Jake. Do you know what's right and what's wrong?"

That was a tricky question. The bishop knew that I had been in trouble several times in Primary. "I know what's right and what's wrong, but sometimes I choose to do what's wrong. Does that mean I can't be baptized?" Now I was worried!

"Everyone makes mistakes, Jake. One of the promises Heavenly Father makes when you get baptized is that He will forgive you when you make mistakes, if you repent. Do you know what repentance is?"

"My Primary teacher says it's like a big eraser. When we have done something we know we shouldn't do, we pray to Heavenly Father and ask Him to forgive us, and promise to try to never do it again. Then that mistake is erased."

The bishop smiled. "And that's Heavenly Father's part of the covenant."

"What's a covenant?"

"I thought you might not know that word. It's when you make a promise and Heavenly Father makes a promise. Heavenly Father's promise is to forgive you when you repent. Do you know what your baptismal promise is?"

"I think my promise is to follow Jesus and to do what He would want me to do."

"That's it. And do you know when you will make the promise again, after you're baptized?"

"No."

"Every Sunday when you take the sacrament, listen to the prayers the priests say. They will remind you of your promises."

That was something I didn't know. I hadn't ever really listened to the prayers. I was going to listen the next Sunday.

"Well, Jake, I think you're ready to be baptized. Let's go see if Jenny is ready for her interview."

That was the end of my interview. And, of course, Jenny passed her interview too. We were both ready to be baptized and we could hardly wait!

THE BIRTHDAY PARTY

We never go to school on Wednesday afternoons. We call it *half-day* because we go to only half a day of school. In the other half of the day the teachers get lessons ready to teach us for another week. I love Wednesdays. It leaves more time to play.

One Wednesday was even better than usual. Jenny and I were going to have our birthday party. Mom had let us invite four friends each—ten second-graders would be plenty for a party, she said. I knew it would be a great party. We were planning to go to the swimming pool and then home, where a clown was going to show us some tricks. After that, we would have ice cream and cake and open our presents.

The only bad part about the party was that Jenny was inviting girls. We've always had our parties together, but lately I've started to not like girls. Don't get me wrong. I still love Mom and Grandma. Jenny's great for a twin sister, and Monica and Doodles are still okay, but other girls, especially girls my age, are starting to give me the creeps.

I had invited my three best buds that I'd known since I was little, and my new friend, Woody. (That's the name I had decided to call Elwood. The kids at school called him Dumbo; Mrs. Barker and his mom called him Elwood; but I didn't think either one of those names was very nice to call a friend. I told my other friends to call him Woody too.)

Our friends all came with their towels and swimming suits. We had to stay in the shallow end of the pool. Mom watched from the bleachers and tried to hold Doodles while we were swimming.

I had brought a penny. We threw the penny in the water and then dived for it. Woody kept getting water up his nose and choking on the water. Then he'd come up and sneeze. The girls laughed at him, but I've had water up my nose and I know how it feels. I told him to hold his nose with one hand and swim with the other. He tried it and it worked much better.

We got to swim for only an hour, so it wasn't long until it was time to go.

Bongo the clown was there when we got home. She had a huge bunch of orange hair and wore green and white clown clothes. Her shoes went way out from her feet—almost two feet long—and they flopped and flipped as she walked. She pulled quarters out of all our ears and gave them to us. Then she changed her quarter into a dime and then into a penny. We couldn't figure out how she was doing it.

When it was time for us to blow out the candles on our cake, Bongo said she had some special candles for me. Everyone sang "Happy Birthday" to Jenny, and she made a wish and blew out her candles. Then they all sang "Happy Birthday" to me, and I made a wish and blew out my candles . . . except that they lit right back up again. Everyone laughed. It was funny, and I laughed too, but then I thought I hadn't blown hard enough, so I took another big breath and blew hard twice in a row. The candles lit right up again. Jenny laughed and said I was blowing so hard my freckles were disappearing into my red face.

I knew I had been tricked. I asked Bongo what the candles were made of, but she was laughing so much she had a hard time talking. When she caught her breath, she said, "They're trick candles, Jake. No one can blow them out. They just keep staying on and staying on. But you've been such a good sport that I'm going to check your head for extra money."

I grinned and said, "Check my head for what?"

"Extra money. People have to be extra smart to be good sports. And you laughed right along with us. You must have some extra money in your head."

She told me to stand up. She lifted up a small bucket and tipped my head so that my ear was inside of it. Then she told me to shake my leg. When I did that, quarters fell out of my ear into the bucket! There was a whole pile of them. I guess it looked and sounded so funny that everyone started laughing again. I hadn't felt anything come out of my ear, but when I felt inside it I guess Bongo had cleaned me out because there were no more quarters.

She handed me the little bucket and started blowing up long balloons and twisting them into animals. Each kid got to choose the animal he wanted. I got a blue giraffe and Jenny got a long pink dog. Then Bongo was done. She waved good-bye to us all and flip-flopped out of the door. We were sorry to see her go, but now it was time to open our presents.

Jenny got to open hers first. She got some doll clothes, a T-shirt, a box of sixty-four crayons with a sharpener in it, and some bows for her hair. I was glad I wasn't a girl. Her presents didn't look like much fun to me.

When it was my turn, I got some really neat presents. I got some matchbox cars, a bubble-gum machine, a hundred-piece puzzle; and Woody gave me a pencil. It was from the pencil machine at school. I had started in kindergarten getting a pencil every week. I didn't use them for school: they were my professional football team pencil collection. I had all of the teams except the Rams, and Woody knew it. As soon as I opened it I checked to see what team it was. "Hey, a Ram's pencil. It's great, Woody. Thanks!"

Jenny looked at me as if I were crazy. She doesn't like Woody much, and probably thought a pencil was a dumb birthday present. But girls don't understand about pencil collections.

Mom drove all our friends home, and that was the end of our birthday party. It had been fun. Only three more days until we were going to get baptized! I could hardly wait!

BAPTISM DAY

Bright and early Saturday morning Uncle Jerry picked Jenny up in his new van. Uncle Jerry uses hand controls to drive because his legs don't work. I love riding in his van, but that morning it was Jenny's turn. When she ran down the steps to get in the van, she was in her swimming suit. She was gone before I could ask her why, but Mom explained that Uncle Jerry and Jenny were going to wash his wheelchair at the car wash. The chair had to be really clean to go into the baptismal font. I thought that was neat!

Uncle John was going to meet us at the church at eleven. He was going to show me exactly how to hold my hands. He didn't want me to be wondering when I went into the font.

Mom made me take a shower. I told her that

didn't make any sense, since I was just going to get wet again when I got baptized. If I had had my way, for the same reason I wouldn't even have combed my hair; it was just going to get messed up when I got baptized. But Mom said if Uncle Jerry's wheelchair needed a shower, I certainly did. I took a shower. I guess it could have been worse. When Jenny got home from the car wash, she had to have a shower and then have her hair curled. Moms are sure funny sometimes.

When we got to the church, Uncle John was waiting. He took me into another room and showed me how to hold my nose as I went under. He showed me in his scriptures exactly what he was going to say to baptize me. He said that every word had to be just right, and that two people called witnesses would listen and make sure he got it just right and then watch and make sure that I went completely under the water. If I didn't, I'd have to be baptized all over again.

I didn't even know there were closets in the hall by the Primary room, but a lady gave us white clothes out of the closet. Uncle John and I got dressed in those clothes and I was all ready to be baptized.

We all went into the Primary room. It was pretty nearly filled up. Jenny and I had our bishop, our Primary president, our Aunt Jody, our Grandma Tolson, Mom, Dad, Doodles, Monica, and the uncles who were going to baptize us—and even Woody and his mom had come. I had invited them, but I hadn't known whether they would be there for sure.

After an opening song, an opening prayer, and two talks about baptism, the bishop called out my name to be the first one baptized. Jenny was glad I was going to be first. She and Uncle Jerry hadn't practiced and she didn't know what to do.

Uncle John and I went through the dressing room and opened the door to the baptismal font. As I stepped in I could feel how warm the water was. It wasn't too cold and wasn't too hot. I smiled as I thought of the next line from Goldilocks: it was just right.

The water came up to my chest. First Uncle John got me in the right position and held my wrist with his left hand. Then he raised his right arm, called me by name, and said, "Having been commissioned of Jesus Christ, I baptize you in the name of the Father, and of the Son, and of the Holy Ghost. Amen." I squeezed my nose and went under the water. At least, most of me went under the water. The bishop said my toe had come up out of the water, so Uncle John had to say and do everything over again. This second time I went all the way under the water—it was all done right. When I came up I felt warm all over; not just on the outside, but all over my insides.

Uncle John and I got out of the font. I held the door open for Uncle Jerry. Uncle John and another dad dressed in white lifted Uncle Jerry in his chair into the baptismal font. Mom had taken Jenny through her dressing room, and she now went down into the font. Uncle Jerry winked at her as she got into the warm water. He placed her hands in the right position, called her by name, said the same words that Uncle John had used in my baptism, leaned way over in his wheelchair, and baptized Jenny. She only had to go under once.

When she came up out of the water she grinned

at me and I grinned back. I knew that Jesus and Heavenly Father were pleased that day because we were members of The Church of Jesus Christ of Latter-day Saints.

WOODY COMES
TO CHURCH

The next day was Sunday—fast Sunday, in fact. In our family we don't fast until we're eight years old and have been baptized. That Sunday was not only the day I was going to be confirmed but was also the first day I was fasting. I thought I was going to starve, but I still wanted to fast. Mom said that we could eat when we got home.

After the opening prayer in sacrament meeting the bishop said it was time to confirm Jenny and me. He said we were going to go in alphabetical order. We had learned about A-B-C order in school this year. The *a* in Jake comes before the *e* in Jenny, so I got to go first. Jenny was glad I kept winning first place no matter how the choosing was done. She was so nervous she wanted to watch me do every-thing first so that she wouldn't be so nervous on her turn. She didn't want to make any mistakes in front of everyone.

I went up to the front and sat on a chair. Uncle Jerry, Uncle John, Brother Henderson, and the bishopric put their hands on my head. When I had watched other kids get confirmed, I had wondered if their heads got tired in holding up all those hands, but when it was my turn I found out they didn't lean on your head, so it wasn't heavy. It just felt a little funny to have all those hands on my head at the same time.

When Uncle John said, "we say unto you, receive the Holy Ghost," I felt a wonderful warm feeling all over my body. It felt really good, and I wondered if I'd always feel that way. Then Uncle John gave me a nice blessing. I don't remember a lot of it, but I do remember that he blessed me that I would be able to go on a mission. I wondered what Dad would think about that. I do want to go on a mission. I hope it's a mission to Russia!

When he said "Amen" I stood up and shook hands with everyone in the circle. Then it was Jenny's turn. She had the same men in her circle and Uncle Jerry confirmed her. I could tell that she was feeling really good when she sat down beside me.

She hadn't made any mistakes when she had been confirmed, but she made a mistake during the sacrament. When Uncle Jerry passed her the bread she didn't take it, but passed the tray right on to me. I took a piece of bread and passed the tray to Mom.

Uncle Jerry leaned over and asked her why she hadn't taken the sacrament. She said she was fasting and didn't want to break her fast. I hadn't even thought of that—her brain sure works differently than mine. But Uncle Jerry said the sacrament was the only food that didn't break your fast. I had Mom pass the bread back to me so that Jenny could have her piece.

After the tray was passed back to Mom, Jenny and I each opened the zipper on the holder of our new scriptures that Grandma Tolson had given us for our baptism. (My scripture case was black and Jenny's was blue, so we wouldn't get them mixed up.) I had put in the side pocket the picture of Jesus that the Primary president had given us during our interview for baptism. She had said that we should take the picture out during the sacrament and think about Jesus. She'd told us that when we have decisions to make we should try to think of how Jesus would decide.

I tried to think what it would have been like if I had been a little boy when Jesus was on the earth. I looked at the little boy standing beside Jesus in the picture. I decided to pretend that I was the boy in the picture. It made me feel good all over.

When sacrament meeting was over Jenny and I walked to the back of the chapel on the way to Primary. There, sitting on the back bench right by the door, were Woody and his mom. I was really excited to see them. "I didn't know you had come," I told them.

Mrs. Blackendorf asked if we were going home right then. I told her that the kids would go to Primary and asked if Woody could go with us. I hoped he could—I knew he would like Primary even better than sacrament meeting. Primary was always fun. Anyway, she said he could come with us. She stayed with my mom in the chapel for their Sunday School.

When it was time to sing the "Hello" song to the visitors, I took Woody up in front of everyone. The boys in the Blazer class in the back laughed when they saw him. I knew what they were thinking. They were thinking that his ears were really big and that his clothes weren't very nice. That's what I had thought when I first met him. But now that I knew him, I knew that his ears and his clothes really didn't count for anything. I knew that ears and clothes don't make any difference to Heavenly Father, nor Jesus, either. It's too bad that it made a difference to the Blazers.

CHAPTER

CUB SCOUTS

Sister Leo had called Mom after my birthday and asked if I was ready to go to Cub Scouts. She said she was the den leader and they met on Wednesday afternoons. It seemed that the next Wednesday would never come. It was great being eight!

Woody was already eight, and when Mom asked Sister Leo about it she said they would love to have Woody come with me. Sister Leo's house, where the Cub Scouts met, was right across the street from the school, but Scouts didn't start until one o'clock, and school was out at twelve-thirty, so Woody, Nathan, and I decided to play on the playground until one.

Nathan said he had to be careful, because he had just had the cast taken off of his arm that morning. In fact, he had been late to school because of his doctor's appointment. I thought being late to school on a half-day would be great. All he had to do was art, and then it was time to go home. How lucky can a guy be?

Nathan had broken his arm when he fell off his skateboard. He belonged to the "Broken Arm Club" at school. It wasn't really a club, but our principal, Mrs. Freckleton, had said he belonged to that club because he and three other kids at our school had all broken their arms the same week. Pam had broken both of her arms by falling off the top of the slide at the park, and she had both arms in casts. She didn't even have to do any school work because she couldn't write. That's one club I'd like to join.

On the far corner of our playground, on the side of the school where the fourth, fifth, and sixth graders play, is a merry-go-round. Second graders aren't allowed to play on it. Sometimes on Saturdays Mom let us play at the school, so we had been on that side before. And that's where we decided to play that afternoon before Scouts.

The merry-go-round had a pole in the middle and then round metal rails that went from about a foot away from that pole to the edge of the merry-go-round. One Saturday some of the big kids had showed us how to "walk the middle" of the merry-go-round. They said this was against the school rules because it was kind of dangerous. But now it wasn't school time, and when we looked around we couldn't see anyone watching, so we decided to try it ourselves.

Woody and I wanted to walk the middle, which makes the merry-go-round spin really fast. Nathan said he would take the first ride. To have a ride, you stand on the outside of the merry-go-round and wait until it goes really fast. Then you grab onto one of the bars as it spins. The older kids that showed us how to do it got great rides when they grabbed the bar. Nathan said his arm would be okay if he just grabbed the bar with his good arm.

We started to walk the middle and got it going faster and faster. Nathan said we had it going so fast that all he could see was a blur where the bars were. But he said he thought he could put his arm out and grab a bar when it hit him.

He grabbed it the very first time he tried. He was screaming with a grin on his face as the speed made his body shoot straight out from the merry-go-round. He held on while the merry-go-round went around almost twice, and then I guess he couldn't hold on anymore even though he was using both hands. But he didn't just let go and fall off onto the ground. He flew kind of like he was Superman flying backwards. It looked so funny that Woody and I laughed as he flew; then we stopped laughing as he landed.

It took us a little while to slow the merry-go-round so we could get off. As soon as we could, we ran over to see if Nathan was all right. He was sitting on the blacktop rubbing his head. We could see that his elbow was bleeding. When he started talking to us, he wasn't making a whole lot of sense; he said really goofy things, and he even asked me what my name was. I was scared. I knew we were going to be in big trouble if anyone knew we had been walking the middle of the merry-go-round.

We thought if we let him sit for a minute he would get better, but when I looked at my watch it was already one o'clock. It was time for Scouts.

Woody took one side of Nathan and I took the other. We put his arms around our shoulders and helped him walk across the street to Sister Leo's. As soon as she opened the door, she knew something was wrong. "Jake, what happened?"

I didn't want to get into trouble, so I said: "I don't know, Sister Leo. Woody and I were just walking across the playground and found him sitting on the blacktop. His elbow is hurt and he says his head hurts too. He's acting really goofy."

The minute the lie was out of my mouth I felt awful inside. It was the first time I had really done something wrong since I was baptized, and when I thought about that it made me feel even worse. I looked at Woody and I could tell that he wasn't feeling so good, either. Oh, why had we walked the middle of the merry-go-round! That was wrong; and now I had told a lie, and that was wrong too.

Sister Leo told Nathan to lie down on the couch and she called his mom. It wasn't long before Nathan's mom came to pick him up. She said she was taking him to the hospital emergency room. She asked us if we were sure we didn't know anything about what had happened. We both shook our heads—no. Another lie. I thought I couldn't feel more awful than I was feeling inside at that moment.

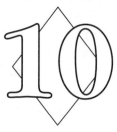

CHANGING AN AWFUL FEELING

Scouts would have been fun if my lies hadn't blocked out all the fun feelings. We made bird-houses out of big plastic pop bottles. Sister Leo even gave us some bird seed to take home, to see if we could get some birds eating out of our birdhouses before winter set in.

She also gave us some of those little pink, brown, and yellow bar cookies that I always eat the outsides of before I eat the middle. But I didn't feel much like eating anything.

On the way home, Woody and I talked about what we had done. I knew he wasn't a baptized member of Jesus' church, so he hadn't promised to remember what Jesus would do and try to do it. But he and his mom were having the missionaries teach them about the Church. I hadn't set a very good ex-ample for him, and that made me feel even worse.

"We shouldn't have lied, Woody."

"I know" was all he said.

I knew I needed to repent. When our Primary teacher had taught us about repentance, she said we didn't just need to tell Heavenly Father we were sorry. We also needed to make sure we had put things right with other people. I knew that Nathan's mom needed to be told how Nathan had become hurt. She and Nathan might still be at the hospital, but I couldn't just drop in and tell her, since the hospital wasn't in our section of town. I knew I had to tell Mom what had happened.

Mom was changing Doodles's diaper when Woody and I got to my house. My heart was pounding; and I guess Satan didn't want me to do the right thing, because I kept thinking, "It won't make any difference if you tell the truth . . . except that you'll be in big trouble for walking the middle of the merry-go-round."

I did care if I got into trouble, but I didn't care about getting in trouble as much as I cared about getting rid of the awful feeling that had settled inside me. I knew there was only one way to get rid of it.

"Mom?" I said it quietly as Mom lifted Doodles over her shoulder. Mom didn't hear me, but Doodles saw me and said, "Ja-kee! Ja-kee!" (That's what she calls me, and I kind of like it.)

Mom turned around and said, "Oh, Jake, I didn't see you come in. How did you and Woody like your first day at Cub Scouts?"

I held up my birdhouse, but I guess she noticed I was being too quiet. "Is something wrong, Jake?" she asked.

"Mom, I've done something really wrong; and

then I lied about it, but I was afraid I was going to get in trouble, and now I feel awful."

"Of course you feel awful. That's the Holy Ghost letting you know you've done something wrong. Remember that good feeling after you were baptized and confirmed that you told me about? You've shooed that good feeling away. But I'm sure it's something that can be put right. Let's go into the front room, and you can tell me all about it."

I felt better already. I knew Mom could make everything all right. I told her everything, about walking the middle of the merry-go-round, about lying to Sister Leo, and about lying to Nathan's mom. I didn't leave anything out, because I knew that if I did I wouldn't get that good feeling back. Woody stood and listened to everything. He didn't say anything, but he nodded his head several times while I told the story.

Mom hurried to the phone and called Nathan's house. No one was home, so she called the hospital. When Nathan's mom came to the phone, Mom told her all about how Nathan got hurt. His mom said that Nathan had a concussion, which Mom told us later was like a bruise on his brain. The doctor said Nathan needed to stay in the hospital until he stopped talking goofy. And he hadn't just skinned his elbow—he had re-broken his arm. Another cast was being put on his arm while his mom talked to my mom. He was back in the Broken Arm Club.

Mom told us everything. Then she said: "Riding the middle of the merry-go-round wasn't a sin. You all three made a wrong choice, because you knew it was dangerous and you did it anyway. But lying to get yourself out of trouble was wrong. And one lie usually leads to another. I'm very glad you decided

40

that what you were doing was only causing you more trouble. You made the right decision to come and talk to me, and I'm proud of both of you." She hugged both Woody and me as she was talking. "Nathan's mom said she's happy that she knows what happened. It's cleared up a lot of questions."

Woody and I played for the rest of the afternoon. That night I told Heavenly Father all about what had happened and told Him that I would try really hard not to tell another lie. After my prayer I lay in bed thinking. I thought about how good it had felt to choose the right and how rotten it had felt to choose wrong. I decided that from then on I was going to be very careful to hang on to that good feeling.

CHAPTER

BOBCATS

Sister Leo had told Woody and me that if we passed off all our Bobcat trail in our Cub Scout book we could get our Bobcat badge at the pack meeting the next Wednesday evening. We decided to work on our badge the next afternoon after school.

We both had a book. We turned to the part that said, "Bobcat Trail." It said there were seven things we had to do.

We studied the Cub Scout Promise and about the Law of the Pack and told Mom what they both meant. She signed both the books. Then we told her that Webelos means "We'll be loyal Scouts" and that the Webelos Arrow of Light points the right way to go every day of the week. We told her the motto was "Do your best," and she signed the fourth paw and we filled it in.

We showed her the Cub Scout sign and told her what it meant; then she signed paw number 5.

We learned the Cub Scout salute, and the handshake with our first two fingers along the inside of each other's wrists, and Mom filled in track numbers 6 and 7.

Now we had all seven tracks filled in. We were going to be Bobcats and have a Bobcat badge on our Cub Scout uniforms!

Pack meeting was held in the Primary room at the church. Mom and Dad and Jenny all came to see me get my Bobcat. Woody's mom brought him, and we all sat together on the second row.

We had the flag ceremony and the prayer. Then the Cubmaster, Brother Miller, asked Woody, me, and our moms to come up to the front. When we had done this, he said: "It's tradition in our pack to welcome our new Bobcats in with a painted Bobcat ceremony. We have two new Bobcats today, and they have worked hard this past week to be ready to take on the colors and spirit of Cub Scouting."

He took out a box that contained some big crayons and invited Mom and Mrs. Blackendorf to draw on our faces with them as he told them what to do.

Then he said: "Blue is from the sky. The paw print on your forehead is the spirit of the Bobcat. This reminds you to do your best on the Cub Scout Trail."

We both felt our moms draw a blue paw print on our foreheads. Everyone laughed a little, and I moved my eyebrows up and down because the crayon made my skin itch a bit.

"Yellow is from the sun. The marks under your

eyes will help you see the light of the Cub Scout Trail; and they symbolize the bright spirit of Cub Scouting."

I felt Mom putting big yellow eyelash shapes under both of my eyes.

"White is for purity. The mark on your nose helps you know right from wrong as you go along this Cub Scout Trail."

A white stripe went down my nose. I looked over at Woody. He looked kind of funny but kind of like an Indian warrior, and we grinned at each other.

"Red is for courage. The mark on your chin reminds you to always speak the truth."

I had already learned my lesson about telling the truth, but I felt Mom put a red mark on my chin.

"Green stands for the spirit of nature. The marks on each cheek will guide you to live in harmony with the great outdoors."

This ended the marking of our faces.

"Remember your markings of this night, new Cubs, and have fun along the Cub Scout Trail."

Brother Miller now said each of us new Bobcats could choose one color and with it make one mark on his mother's face. I watched as Woody made a red mark at the end of his mom's nose. I knew exactly what I was going to do. I took out the black crayon and drew a long black mustache that went from Mom's chin, up across her top lip, and down to her chin again. She looked so funny that everyone laughed.

Then they gave each of us a Bobcat pin for his mom, and Brother Miller asked my dad to come up and help him give us our badges. I didn't know why he needed Dad's help until Brother Miller explained that the Bobcat badge is always pinned on the Bobcat upside down. Then when he does a good turn for someone he can turn it right side up and have his mom sew it on his uniform.

Instead of turning the *badge* upside down, our pack always turns the *boy* upside down. Brother Miller and Dad flipped me over and held me upside down while Mom pinned on the badge. Then they put me back on my feet and turned Woody upside down while his mom pinned on his badge.

Jenny told me later that my face was really red while I was upside down. I guess with my red hair and my red face I looked pretty funny. But I didn't care. I was a Bobcat Scout!

THE GREATEST
GOOD TURN

The day started out to be normal enough. While she was in the shower I sneaked into Jenny's room and made her bed. I thought it was a great idea for a good turn. When I told Mom what I'd done, she said she would sew on my Bobcat badge that afternoon. I wondered if Woody had done his good turn as fast as I had. I had no way of knowing that I was going to be part of his good turn in a big way later on that day.

During breakfast I asked Mom if I could go over to Woody's house after school. Jenny looked disgusted and asked, "Jake, why are you always hanging around Dumbo?"

I know she didn't mean to say "Dumbo" out loud. Jenny is so careful not to get in trouble that she doesn't get in trouble very often. But Woody's other nickname had slipped out, and putting her hand over her mouth wasn't going to change that fact.

Mom's eyebrows went down as she turned around and asked, "Jenny, what did you call him?"

"I called him Dumbo—but I didn't mean to. He is weird, though, Mom. He doesn't wear nice clothes, and his ears are big, and, well, I wish he wouldn't come to our church anymore."

I had known that she didn't like Woody. But knowing my mom, I knew that Jenny had just gotten herself into more trouble.

"Jenny," Mom said quietly, "do you have any idea why Elwood doesn't wear nice clothes?"

"No." Her voice was even softer.

"Elwood's dad died of cancer last year. They didn't have any insurance, and they still have doctor bills and hospital bills to pay. They live in an old trailer down by the railroad tracks because they can't afford to live anywhere else. Before Elwood's dad got sick they lived in a nice home across town and had nice clothes. Then they had to move into the trailer, and into our school area."

Then she looked straight at Jenny. "You haven't been mean to him at school or at church, have you?"

"No . . . really I haven't," she said, "but I haven't been very nice to him, either. I don't feel good around him."

"Jenny," Mom said, "could it be because you think mean things about him? You know that the Holy Ghost doesn't help you to feel good when you're not doing the right thing. Jesus says that we need to love everyone."

"*Love!* Mom, I can't love Woody!"

Jenny's eyes were big, and I thought it was kind

of a funny thing for Mom to want her to do, too. But Mom explained. "There are a lot of ways to love people. Do you love me the same way as you love Jake?"

"No."

"Do you love Daddy the same way as you love Monica?"

"No."

"Do you love Doodles the same way as you love your first-grade teacher, Miss Leslie?"

"No."

"Jesus says we are to love everyone, but sometimes that means just to remember that everyone is a child of God. Because you know that, you need to be nice to everyone."

Jenny thought about that for a minute, then I spoke up: "Jenny, I think you'd like Woody if you got to know him. Do you want to play four square with us at recess?" (I wouldn't just invite any old girl to do this, but Jenny wasn't just any old girl. She was my twin, and that made it okay to play with her at recess.)

She said she'd like that and she was really going to try to be friends with Woody.

The rest of the day was a regular day, except that Jenny played with us at recess. On the way in from afternoon recess, she whispered to me, "You were right. Woody is a lot of fun!" That made me really happy.

During recess Jenny told us she would walk us to Woody's trailer after school and then go home. It was a little out of her way, but she said there wasn't anything else she wanted to do.

We were on our way to Woody's trailer when it happened. I still can't believe it. We were walking along and talking. We got to a corner, and Jenny sat down on the curb to tie her shoes. She hadn't said anything, so Woody and I started to walk across the street. We had just gone a couple of steps when we heard the brakes of a car squeal as it tried to stop. I looked up and kind of froze as I saw the car coming towards us. Woody didn't freeze, though, and instead of getting out of the way himself, he shoved me out of the way just before the car was going to hit me. I fell on the road at the same time that I heard a sickening thud. I knew that Woody had been hit by the car. I turned around to see him go up on the hood and then fall onto the road. He didn't move after he fell.

I ran over to Woody and so did Jenny. Then we heard the car squeal again. That time it was the tires squealing. The driver raced the car around us and didn't even stop to help. I know how it feels to not want to get into trouble, and I guess that's how he felt, that's why he left us. But that man was a grown-up, and he had left Jenny and me by ourselves. And we didn't know anything about how to help Woody.

PRAYERS AND TEARS

Woody was lying so still that Jenny and I thought he was dead. There was a bad cut on his forehead, and it was really bleeding. His eyes were closed, and he wasn't even moaning.

I told Jenny I was going to get some help. I ran up the steps and onto the porch of the house on the corner. I didn't know who lived in that house, but there was a car in the driveway, so I thought someone might be home. I started banging hard on the door and kept on banging while I prayed to Heavenly Father. "Please let Woody be okay. Please let Woody be okay." I glanced back to see Jenny sitting beside Woody on the road and knew that she must be praying too. Her arms were folded and her eyes were closed. We were both crying.

I was still banging when I heard a lady say,

"Hold your horses, I'm coming." She opened the door with an angry face and shouted, "What is the matter with you? Can't you give an old woman time to get to the door?"

She was angry, but as soon as she said her angry words she saw I had been crying. She softened her voice and asked me what was wrong. I told her about Woody, and she opened the door wide and told me to run to the phone in the kitchen and dial 911. I ran as she shouted her address to me. It felt good to have someone helping me.

When I had hung up the phone she put her arm on my shoulder and said, "Now let's see what we can do to help your friend before the ambulance comes." I waited for her to walk across the room using her cane and held the door open. I could see that Jenny had found someone to help her too, for there was now a car parked in the middle of the road right in front of Woody. That would keep him safe from other drivers until the ambulance came. I thanked Heavenly Father when I saw whose car it was and who was kneeling over Woody. It was Bishop Lee's wife, and she had covered Woody with a blanket.

It took a few minutes for my lady to get down the steps. By the time we got over to Woody we could hear the ambulance. Just then Woody opened his eyes. Sister Lee told him he needed to lie really still and quiet. She had put her hand right over the cut, pushing hard on his forehead, and this had stopped the bleeding.

It wasn't really cold outside, but Woody was shaking.

The ambulance people brought a board with

straps on it out of the ambulance. They asked Woody where he was hurting. He said he hurt everywhere, but that his leg was *really* hurting.

They replaced Sister Lee's hand with a white piece of material, and she stood up to let the ambulance workers talk to Woody. She put one arm around Jenny and one arm around me. I was glad Sister Lee had been the person in the car.

The ambulance workers were careful with Woody's leg, and they rolled him onto his side and put the board right up behind him. Then they rolled him onto his back so that the board was underneath him. They buckled the straps around him, picked him up, and put him into the ambulance.

The police came just before the ambulance left. They asked Sister Lee to tell them what had happened. She told them she hadn't seen what had happened—that we were the only ones who had seen Woody get hit. They took our names and address and said they would come to our home when our parents were there.

Sister Lee told them she would get Woody's mother and take her to the hospital. We got into her car, and she took us home. She waited in the car until we made sure that Mom was home, and then she went to get Mrs. Blackendorf.

The minute we came in, Mom could tell something was wrong. When she asked us, both Jenny and I started talking, trying to tell Mom everything at once. Mom couldn't understand anything, so she told us both to stop and take a big breath. Then she asked Jenny to tell her what had happened.

Jenny started to tell her, but when she got to the part about Woody saving me she started crying so hard that I had to finish.

When I got through, Mom hugged us both and asked if we would like her to say a prayer with us. We knelt down by the couch right then to thank Heavenly Father for protecting me; then we asked Heavenly Father to watch over Woody at the hospital. It's a good thing Mom was the one giving the prayer. Jenny and I were both crying.

FASTING FOR
A REASON

We didn't hear anything from the hospital that night, but two policemen came to our house after Dad got home from work. They wanted to know if we remembered anything about the car or the man in the car. They said it was against the law to leave after you hurt someone with your car. I thought that was a good law. The man had hurt Woody with the car, and then he had hurt us by leaving us alone when Woody was hurt.

All I could remember was that the car was green. I had only seen the car from the front and only for a second.

But Jenny told them she had been sitting on the curb, and that she had seen the whole car from the side. They asked her if she remembered what shade of green it was.

She told them it was the color of the green peas

you get out of a can. She remembered that it was a station wagon like Sister Lee's, except that it was older and uglier. She said she thought the man didn't take very good care of his car because one of the windows on the side was just a piece of plastic taped over the window with silver tape.

One of the policemen said he had seen a car like that parked at the house next door to Simon's Market. They said they would let us know if they found out anything.

Dad rocked us to sleep that night. It's a game he has played with Jenny and me ever since we were little. Jenny always has the first turn. He rocks her in the big rocking chair and she pretends to go to sleep. Then he always tells Mom, "Oh, dear! Jenny has fallen fast asleep. I guess I'll have to carry her up to bed." She tries not to laugh, but she usually can't help smiling as he carries her up to bed. He tucks her in, gives her a good-night kiss, and tries to sneak out the door. She always says, "Good-night, Daddy," and he laughs a little and says, "Good-night, Princess." That's the signal that it's my turn to be rocked.

He rocks me for a little while and I start to snore loud. It's not just a little loud sound. It's like the snore of the pretend people on cartoons. When I start snoring, Dad says, "I think this one has fallen asleep too; I'd better take him to bed." And he walks up the stairs with me snoring like a pig all the way. It's always hard not to laugh.

This night, Dad and I talked before I snored. He said he was so glad that I hadn't been hurt, and he held me extra close. I wouldn't want my friends to know that my dad still rocked me to sleep. I'm too old for it, but it always makes me feel safe and loved just before I go to sleep. That night, I put my arms around my dad's neck and let him rock me a long time before I snored. Somehow it made me feel a little bit better after that scary day.

Even when I went to bed after my long rocking time I was still wide awake. I had said my prayers with Mom as we always did before Dad rocked us, but I still felt I needed to talk to Heavenly Father. I spent some time talking to Him while I knelt down beside my bed, and then I got into bed without saying amen. I just kept on praying and praying until I fell asleep.

When Mom woke me up in the morning she said she would call Sister Lee before we left for school to find out if she knew anything about Woody. Mom thought Woody's mom would probably have stayed at the hospital all night. There wasn't a phone at Woody's house, anyway.

When Sister Lee answered, she said she had stayed with Mrs. Blackendorf until late the night before. She said the bishop and his counselor had gone to see Woody and had told him about priesthood blessings. Woody had asked if he could have one. They had given him a blessing, and he was soon fast asleep.

The doctors were going to do tests that morning to see what kind of damage had been done. They knew he had a broken leg, and they had stitched up his head. They needed to check to see if anything inside was hurt.

Sister Lee said their family was going to fast for Woody that day and asked if we wanted to join them.

When Mom hung up, she told us what Sister Lee had said. Jake and I asked why fasting would help.

She explained to us that when we have an extra special reason that we want a prayer answered, we can fast. She said fasting is like an extra line put into our call for Heavenly Father's help. He knows how much we want that prayer answered when we add fasting to our prayers.

Jenny and I both asked if we could fast. We knew it would be hard to do this at school, but we really wanted to help Woody. Monica said she would fast; and Mom was going to fast. It felt good to have so many extra lines into Heavenly Father. We were glad we hadn't eaten breakfast yet that morning.

It really wasn't hard to fast through school that day. It was different from the first day we had fasted on the day we were confirmed. I remembered how I had thought about food all day long on that day; I could hardly wait to get home so that I could get something into my stomach. At school this day, though, all I could think about was Woody.

At lunchtime, Mrs. Barker was on outside lunch duty. Jenny and I were the first ones outside, because we weren't eating lunch. Mrs. Barker was sitting on the grass, so we sat down beside her. She asked us how we had gotten finished eating so quickly.

Neither one of us was afraid of Mrs. Barker anymore. She had seemed mean and scary at the first of the year, but now we knew she wasn't really scary at all. It had taken Jenny longer to figure that out than it had taken me.

We told her all about the accident and how Woody had saved me. And we told her that we were fasting for Woody.

Then Jenny told her about Woody's problems before the accident. She told her about his dad and their bills and their trailer. Jenny said she wished there was something we could do to help. Mrs. Barker thought for a minute and then said she would tell Mr. Woodward. He was in charge of the student council. She thought they might come up with something that would help.

That afternoon, in the middle of science, Mrs. Blackendorf came into our class. She looked tired, but she was smiling. She told Mrs. Barker that she had come to get some homework for Elwood. She had just brought him home from the hospital. She said he had a broken leg, and that the cast went from his toes to about six inches above his knee. He would be in a wheelchair for a while, but other than the broken leg and the stitches in his head he was fine. And he would be back to school on Monday.

Jenny and I were so happy we were ready to burst. I knew that Heavenly Father had answered our fasting and prayers. Woody was going to be just fine! I said a quick prayer at my desk. I didn't even close my eyes, but I left them open and looked over at Jenny. I thought maybe she was doing the same thing. We both wanted Heavenly Father to know that we knew who had helped Woody.

A WONDERFUL
ASSEMBLY

We visited Woody several times before Monday.
He was lying on his couch on a blanket every time
we were there. Being in the Broken Arm Club
seemed like fun, but I decided I didn't want to have
anything to do with a broken leg. The only time
Woody got to get off the couch was to go to the
bathroom. He even had a tray to eat on right next to
the couch. I'd go crazy if I had to lie around all day.
It's hard enough trying to sit through math. And
Woody was doing just what I would be doing—he
was going crazy.

I told Mom and she let us buy him a coloring
book, some crayons, and some comic books. He really liked them. And we worked on our Wolf badge,
doing the things we could do sitting down. At least
he had something to do besides watching TV.

Saturday I carried my Monopoly game clear to

his house. By the middle of the game I just knew I was going to beat him. I had houses and motels on most of my property. But I kept landing on Woody's property. It took most of the morning, but Woody finally won the game.

Monday morning, Jenny and I waited outside the school for Mrs. Blackendorf to bring Woody. When she arrived she took a wheelchair out of the trunk of the car and we helped get Woody out of his side of the car into the wheelchair. Mrs. Blackendorf was in her Sunday dress, and she said she was going to stay for an assembly. She said she didn't know what the assembly was about, but the principal had stopped by her home and invited her to be there.

At nine o'clock we all went into the assembly. We have all of our assemblies in the gym. We don't have a stage. We leave our chairs in our rooms and sit on the floor Indian-style. That way we can see people who are standing up.

The two policemen that had come to our house were on chairs in front of the gym with Mrs. Blackendorf, Mr. Woodward, and the student council. I couldn't figure out what was going on. Everyone else was wondering the same thing, so we all quieted down quickly when the student body president asked us to be quiet.

We all said the Pledge of Allegiance, and then Mr. Woodward asked me and Woody to come up to the front. As I was pushing Woody's wheelchair there Mr. Woodward handed the microphone to one of the policemen.

The policeman waited until we were beside him. Then he said: "Last week, Elwood Blackendorf and his friend Jake Jacobs were walking home from school. A car driven by a man who had been drinking came down the street heading right for Jake and Elwood. Elwood didn't even think about what might happen to him. He only thought about his friend Jake. He pushed Jake out of the way, and Jake didn't get hit by the car. But Elwood got hit, and you can see by his stitches and his cast that he got hurt pretty badly.

"Elwood had time to get himself out of danger, but he chose instead to get his friend out of danger. For that reason we would like to give Elwood a special award.

"Every year our city gives awards to citizens who we think have been heroes. We give these awards out as soon as we hear about what they have done, and then we honor them at a banquet at the end of the year. This year we are proud to include Elwood Blackendorf as one of the city's 'Heroes of the Year.' His picture and a plaque will be in the City Hall building in a trophy case reserved for all the heroes we have honored. We will also award another plaque to Elwood so that he can always remember the day he chose to save his friend rather than himself. You should be proud that you know Elwood Blackendorf, one of our city's Heroes of the Year."

He handed Woody a wooden plaque that was gold on the front and had some writing on it. As he did, the sixth-grade students and all the teachers stood up and clapped. And pretty soon everyone was standing and clapping. It wasn't a little clap like we give when we want to be polite. It was a great big sound. Everyone was clapping for Woody. I was trying to clap louder than everyone else. After all, it was me that Woody had saved.

Woody just sat in his wheelchair. His face was bright red. I guess it was kind of embarrassing to have everyone in a school stand up and clap for you. It was kind of like having everyone at your table sing "Happy Birthday" to you at a restaurant while everyone that's not at your table looks at you too.

Mr. Roberts from the newspaper was there to take pictures, and he took a picture of Woody and me together when everyone was clapping. There was an empty chair on the end of the people up in front, and I sat in it during the rest of the assembly. Woody in his wheelchair was right beside me.

Then Mr. Woodward thanked the policemen for coming and said the student council had an idea. He told us that the student body president, Jaren Thomas, would tell us about it.

Jaren told us about how much it costs to go to the hospital. He said the student council didn't think a hero's family should have to pay hospital bills that resulted from his heroism. So they had decided that, starting one week from that day, we should all try to bring all our pennies and nickels to school. He said the student council would bring around a sheet and we would all throw in the pennies and nickels we'd brought. Then Tuesday we should bring our dimes. Wednesday we should bring our quarters, and Thursday we should bring any other money we wanted to give. Then we would have another assembly the next Monday and give the money to Mrs. Blackendorf to help pay for the hospital bills.

Everyone thought it was a great idea. Mrs. Barker had said she thought the student council could come up with a good idea, and she was right.

Then the student council said they had a song they wanted to sing for Woody. They sang, "Did You Ever Know That You're My Hero?" I don't know if that's the name of the song, but those are the important words. They must have practiced for a long time, because they sounded really good.

I looked around the gym while they were singing. My mom was standing up at the back. It didn't surprise me that she was wiping her eyes. Some songs do funny things to my mom. A lot of times they make her cry. Moms sure do cry for a lot of reasons. I guess it's a mom thing.

When the assembly was over, we all went back to our classes. Mrs. Barker told us that maybe we could ask our neighbors for their extra change. And maybe our moms and dads could ask people at their work. We'd have to wait for a week, but I had a feeling that the sheet was going to be really heavy.

A DAY IN COURT

Ever since the accident, Jenny and I had talked a lot about the man who hit Woody with the car. Jenny thought so much about him that she had started having nightmares. In the nightmare the man would drive up in his green car and turn his head and stare at her. She said his eyes were buggy, and he had eyebrows that were black and bushy and always slanted down to the middle. His teeth were big and crooked and yellow. She even said he always had on a half of a smile, as if he wasn't even sorry that he'd hurt Woody.

She really hadn't seen the man. None of us had. But I guess her brain thought that someone who would be mean enough to leave us alone when Woody was hurt would look like a mean man. I told her we ought to call him the Boogie Man, since he was such a scary guy.

Mom had gone up to talk to the policemen after the assembly. The one who gave Woody his plaque had said that our Boogie Man was drunk when he hit Woody with his car. She asked the officer what else he knew.

The policeman said that the day after we had told him about the pea-green car, he and another officer went to the house next door to Simon's Market. The car wasn't there, but a man answered the door. He was drunk, and he yelled at them, "You already picked me up yesterday. Get off of my property and leave me alone!"

The policemen left and went back to the police station to check with the other officers and see who had picked up the man the day before. They found that Officer Dale had stopped the car. He said that at three-forty-five he'd spotted the car driving fast and not very straight. He had pulled the car over, and could tell that the man had been drinking. Officer Dale said that he had taken him down to the police station and made him blow into a machine that showed he'd had way too many drinks to be driving on the road.

He said he had driven the man home and kept his car. The man was going to go to court the next week.

When the two officers put their stories together, they knew they were talking about the same man. It was the man that had hit Woody with a car and had driven away fast. School had let out at three-thirty. Mrs. Barker never lets us leave the room until we "vacuum" it with our hands. Every paper needs to be picked up before we leave. We had left the classroom five minutes late that day. The man must have hit Woody with the car, driven away fast, and been picked up by the other policeman right afterwards.

The policemen told Mom that someone would be contacting us. They wanted us to go to court and tell what we knew about the accident.

Mom told us everything she knew. When she said we had to go to court, Jenny panicked and I got excited. She didn't want to meet the Boogie Man. He was scary enough in her dream. But I wanted to meet the Boogie Man. Imagine, meeting a real Boogie Man! I didn't want to get up close to him, but I wouldn't mind seeing him across the room. I could hardly wait!

The next day we found out we had to go to court on that Friday. Jenny worried all week about meeting the Boogie Man, and I was so excited I could hardly sleep.

Friday morning we got dressed in our Sunday clothes and headed for court. We picked up Woody and his mom on the way. Woody was still in his wheelchair, so Mom had to help get him into the car and then fold up the wheelchair and put it into the trunk. I told her we should have had Uncle Jerry pick us up in his van, but Mom said she thought we could manage Woody's wheelchair with our car.

I looked around when we got into the courtroom. No one there looked like the Boogie Man. Jenny, Woody, and I decided to play a game. We called it Spot the Boogie Man, and the winner was going to be the one who saw the Boogie Man first.

There were a lot of people there that we didn't know. There was a man in the front sitting with another man. A lady in a green dress sat behind him with two big boys who looked as if they were in high school.

Everyone had to stand up when the judge came in. Then the judge sat down and so did we. He looked at some papers and then asked one of the men on the front row some questions.

Mom leaned over and whispered that the man who had just spoken was the man who was driving the car that hit Woody. It wasn't fair. Mom had just won the game, and the Boogie Man was a regular-looking guy. We would never have guessed. I leaned over and whispered to Jenny, "bushy eyebrows, yellow teeth . . . some dreamer you are." She just shrugged her shoulders and gave me a little grin.

There was a lot of talking that we didn't understand. Then we took turns telling what we remembered. I spoke first. It was neat. I got to go up to the chair by the judge, just like on TV. From that chair up front I got a good eyeball-to-eyeball look at the Boogie Man. I was disappointed. My chance to see a real Boogie Man had fizzled. He didn't look any more like a mean guy than my dad did.

Then it was Woody's turn. His mom just wheeled him up to the front, and then when he was finished Jenny told what she could remember.

Finally, the judge decided what would happen to the man. It sounded as if he were speaking a language from another country. I didn't understand any of it and decided I'd have to ask Mom later.

We all stood up again when the judge left. Then the lady behind the man put her hand on his shoulder. Mom said, "That must be his wife and children. They have really been through a lot of pain, too."

Boogie Men weren't supposed to have a wife and kids. They live behind garbage cans and under beds. This man not only looked regular, he had a regular life.

All of a sudden, the Boogie Man came towards us, holding his wife's hand. His head was down and he was looking at the floor, but he was walking right toward us. Jenny leaned closer to Mom, but I wasn't scared of him anymore.

"I know this won't help much, but I want you to know that I am so sorry for the pain I have caused you. When I drink, I don't think right . . ." and the Boogie Man started to cry. "I would never hurt anyone on purpose, or leave two kids by themselves to look after someone I had hurt. I'm just not like that."

He looked up at Mom and Mrs. Blackendorf. Tears were rolling down his cheeks. "I hope you can find it in your hearts someday to forgive me."

He looked at Mrs. Blackendorf. "I'm glad the judge said that the money I will pay to the court for my fine will be given to you to help pay for your son's hospital bill."

Mom said something about wishing him luck on getting his alcoholism under control. They talked for a few more minutes and he and his wife and boys left the courtroom.

"Mom," Jenny asked, "what is alcoholism?"

"Jenny," she explained, "do you remember what the Word of Wisdom tells us about drinking strong drink?"

"Yes. We're not supposed to."

"Well, Heavenly Father knew it would be harmful to our bodies. Alcohol is a drug. And some people who take one drink want another drink and then another. Their bodies just keep telling them to get another drink and another and another. They use up all their money, lose their jobs, and cause a lot of trouble for their families. They find themselves doing things because of the alcohol that they normally wouldn't do. The alcohol makes it so that they really can't think right."

"You mean," Jenny asked, "that man might really be a nice man if he weren't drinking so much?"

"That's exactly right, Jenny. Alcohol changes people. If that man had never taken a drink, he probably would have been able to stop before he hit Woody. And even if he couldn't, he wouldn't have left you alone to take care of Woody."

The Boogie Man really was a regular man, and he'd messed up just like a regular man. As much as I'd messed up in my eight years, I wondered if I'd ever mess up this big when I was older. I decided that I'd never ever take a drink that had alcohol in it. Heavenly Father said it wasn't good for us. I knew now that it wasn't only bad for our bodies but was bad for our families too.

"Mom," I asked, "Heavenly Father's repentance eraser works for everyone, doesn't it?"

"Yes, it does, Jake. Heavenly Father loves that man every bit as much as He loves you and me. Isn't it nice to know that He loves us even when we make mistakes?"

I nodded my head. She was right. That was a nice thing to know. Especially for a kid like me who was bound to make lots of mistakes.

FRIENDS FOREVER

The fund-raising plan was exciting to watch. Every day four of the student body officers would come into our classroom holding a sheet at each of its four corners. They had already been to the kindergarten rooms and the first grade rooms. They would go in order until they were finished walking through the rooms of all six grades of our school.

The first day it looked as if all the kids had cleared out their piggy banks. The sheet was already sagging when they came to our classroom. We threw our pennies and nickels into the sheet. Jenny and I had been around our block, and all the neighbors seemed to be happy to give us all their change when we told them what we were going to use it for.

Some of our class had butter bowls full of pennies; some, plastic bags. Jenny and I had a canful. Mrs. Barker had a huge bottle. It took her a while to dump all the pennies out of it. She said she had been saving them for twenty years and that she couldn't think of a better way to spend them.

The student body officers told our class that when they got finished with the sixth grade classes they would come back to show Woody how much they had gathered in the sheet from all of the grades.

About thirty minutes later we heard some noise and some laughter down the hall. We all looked up in time to see Mr. Woodward and the four student body officers trying to drag a sheet full of pennies and nickels through our doorway. There was no way that they could lift the sheet. It was too full.

We all clapped and cheered, and Woody raised his fist in the air and shouted, "All right!"

They dragged the sheet back through the door and said they would count the money that night and let us know Tuesday morning how much had been gathered on Monday.

On Tuesday the same student body officers came to our classroom. They said they had stayed with Mr. Woodward and the principal until nine o'clock the night before rolling the pennies and nickels and counting them. They wanted to know if any of us had mothers who would be willing to help count the money every evening after school.

They said we wouldn't believe how much money had been gathered. We knew it would be a lot, but when they said they had counted $513.42 the night before, we went crazy. (We weren't crazy, though, for very long. Mrs. Barker was still Mrs. Barker.)

We threw our dimes into the sheet. The student body officers continued through the classrooms and ended up in our classroom again after their rounds.

Again, the sheet was heavy. And it was heavy on

71

Wednesday. It wasn't so heavy on Thursday, but instead of only change there were lots of dollar bills. I saw one-dollar bills, a twenty, some fives, and some checks. We couldn't wait until the next Monday to see how much money had been thrown into the sheet in all.

On Sunday the missionaries came to our house. They had been to our home for dinner a couple weeks before, so we knew their names. They were Elder Monson and Elder Johnson. I had gotten the giggles when I had first heard their names. They had laughed right along with me and had said, "call us the rhyming missionaries."

They had a surprise for us. Woody and his mom were going to get baptized!

I had never thought about a big person getting baptized. Everyone I had seen baptized had been eight years old. I decided that was something I would like to watch. It was also something I hadn't thought about getting ready for when the time came to get ready to go on my mission. I'd have to make sure I was really strong. If I had to baptize a dad, I would really have to have muscles.

The missionaries said Bishop Lee was going to baptize both Woody and his mother. He had been the one to give Woody a blessing at the hospital. They said Mrs. Blackendorf had felt something special while the bishop was giving the blessing. The missionaries had given her a Book of Mormon the week before the accident, but she hadn't even started to read it. That night, when she got home from the hospital, she started to read the Book of Mormon. It was difficult for her to stop reading the book, and when she finished it she prayed about it and knew it was true.

Woody and his mom would be baptized the Saturday after Woody had his cast removed.

On Monday the assembly to give Mrs. Blackendorf and Woody the money that had been thrown onto the sheet was going to begin at two.

At one-fifty the fire alarm sounded. Mrs. Barker grabbed her roll book, hit the button on her stopwatch, and turned off the lights as we headed out of our door. We have a place on the lower playground where we line up in A-B-C order. It's mostly blacktop and is away from the building.

I love fire drills. I always hope it's a real fire. That would really be exciting! Mrs. Barker always times us. We see how fast we can get in line. Then Mrs. Barker calls roll, and when Angela Washington (the last name on our roll) says, "Here," Mrs. Barker hits the stop button.

That day, the fire drill was even more exciting. Woody had said, "Oh, no!" when he heard the fire bell ring. I looked over at him and could see what he meant. It would be different trying to beat the clock with Woody in a wheelchair, but I told him not to worry; I'd help him.

Most of the kids were already out the door by the time I pushed Woody out and bounced him down the one step outside the door. Then we were off.

I started running him down the sidewalk. Woody was hollering, "Look out below," as we picked up speed. I was running so fast trying to keep up with the wheelchair on the sloping sidewalk that led down to the lower playground that I just decided to hop a ride. There are bars on the bottom of the wheelchair that were just right to ride on, so I jumped on and had the ride of my life.

I could hear some noise behind me, and Woody

and I were making a lot of noise of our own as we screamed down our homemade roller coaster. Everyone moved out of the way, and we made it down to the blacktop in record time.

We turned around to see if everyone else was coming, and everyone was running with Mrs. Barker. I didn't know Mrs. Barker could run. She didn't look very happy, and Woody said that now we were really going to get it. I told him the ride was worth getting into trouble. He agreed and we laughed for a second, then wiped off our smiles when Mrs. Barker ran up. She was breathing so hard that she could hardly catch her breath. I worried for a minute that she was going to have a heart attack.

With her angry face she looked back and forth at Woody and me. We gave her a little smile and she started calling roll. When she hit the stop button, we had beaten the old record by five seconds! (Mrs. Barker had always been the last one to come to the blacktop. She had never run all the way before.)

The bell rang again to tell us to go back to class. We found out later that a sixth grader had been playing with the fire alarm. He got into so much trouble that he probably won't do that again.

But all that happened to Woody and me was that Mrs. Barker made us promise not to race like that again. She said Woody already had one broken leg and he didn't need the rest of his body broken.

We were ten minutes late for the assembly. But it was probably best. Mrs. Barker said that since we'd had a break, our wiggles should be out of us.

Mr. Woodward spoke first. He reminded us of our assembly a few weeks before. Then he asked Mrs. Blackendorf and Woody to come to the front.

The student body president came forward carrying a huge envelope. Mr. Woodward handed him the microphone.

He said, "On behalf of all the students of East Elementary, we would like to present you with this check to be used to help pay your son's hospital bills."

Mrs. Blackendorf thanked him as she took the big envelope. They had made a huge check so that she could hold it up and show everyone. But she didn't turn it around at first. She just stared at it, and her lip started to tremble. By the time she turned it around, she was really crying. I knew that grownups do that sometimes when they're really happy.

When she turned the check around and held it up, we could see that it was for $2,452.32. No wonder she was crying!

I sat there thinking about my friend Woody. I hadn't even known him at the first of the year; and now, I wouldn't even have been here if he hadn't saved my life. That made him the best friend I'd ever had. As everyone stood and clapped and cheered, I looked at him and he looked at me, and I knew that Elwood J. Blackendorf and I would be friends forever.

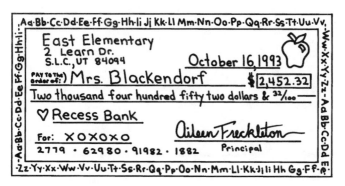

75

ABOUT THE AUTHOR

Bette Molgard received a bachelor's degree from Utah State University in elementary education. She has taught preschool, seminary, special education, and second-grade classes, and has worked to establish one of the first Parent Education Resource centers in the state of Utah. She is the coauthor of several activity books for children.

The author and her husband, Max H. Molgard, are the parents of six children. The family resides in Tooele, Utah.